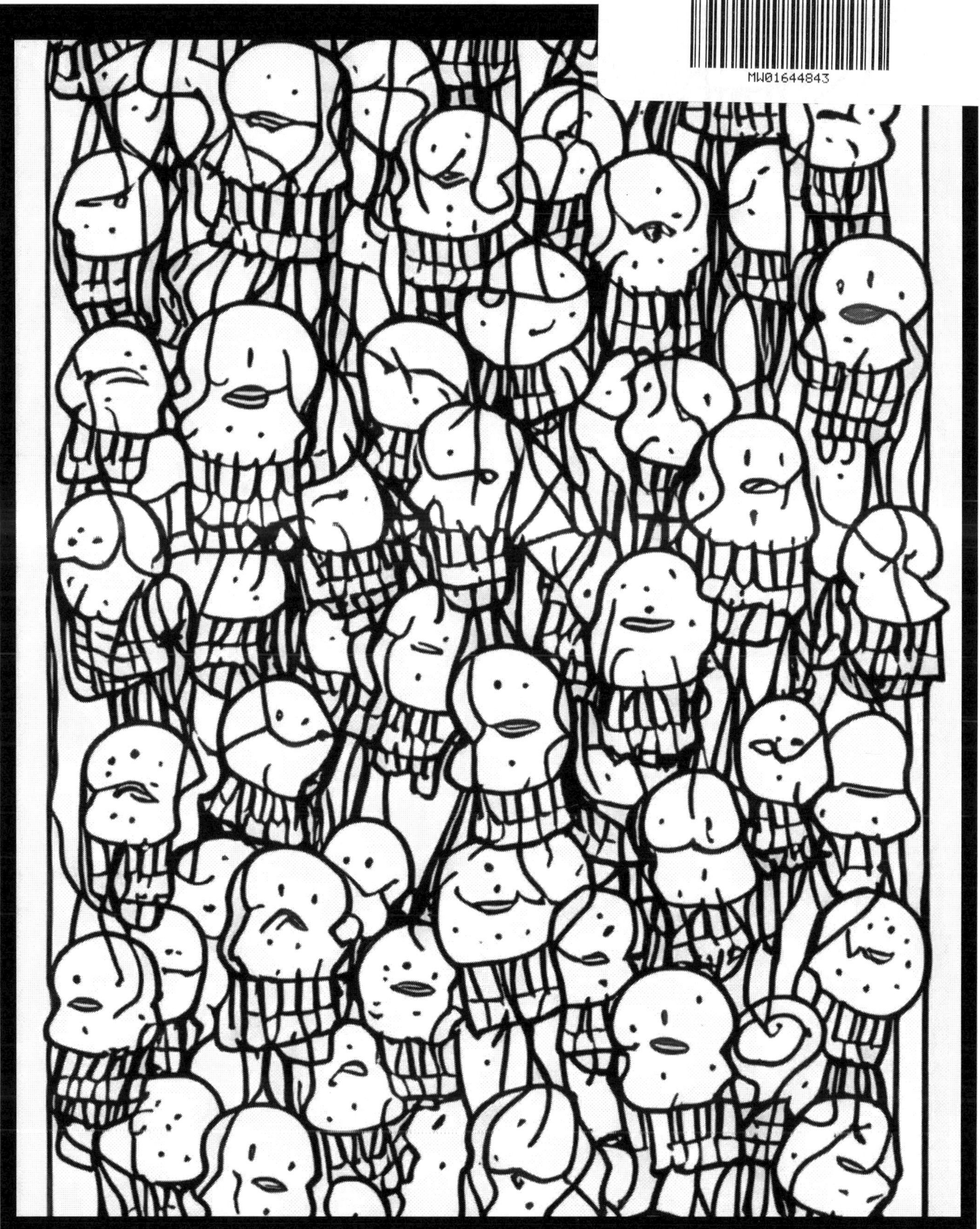

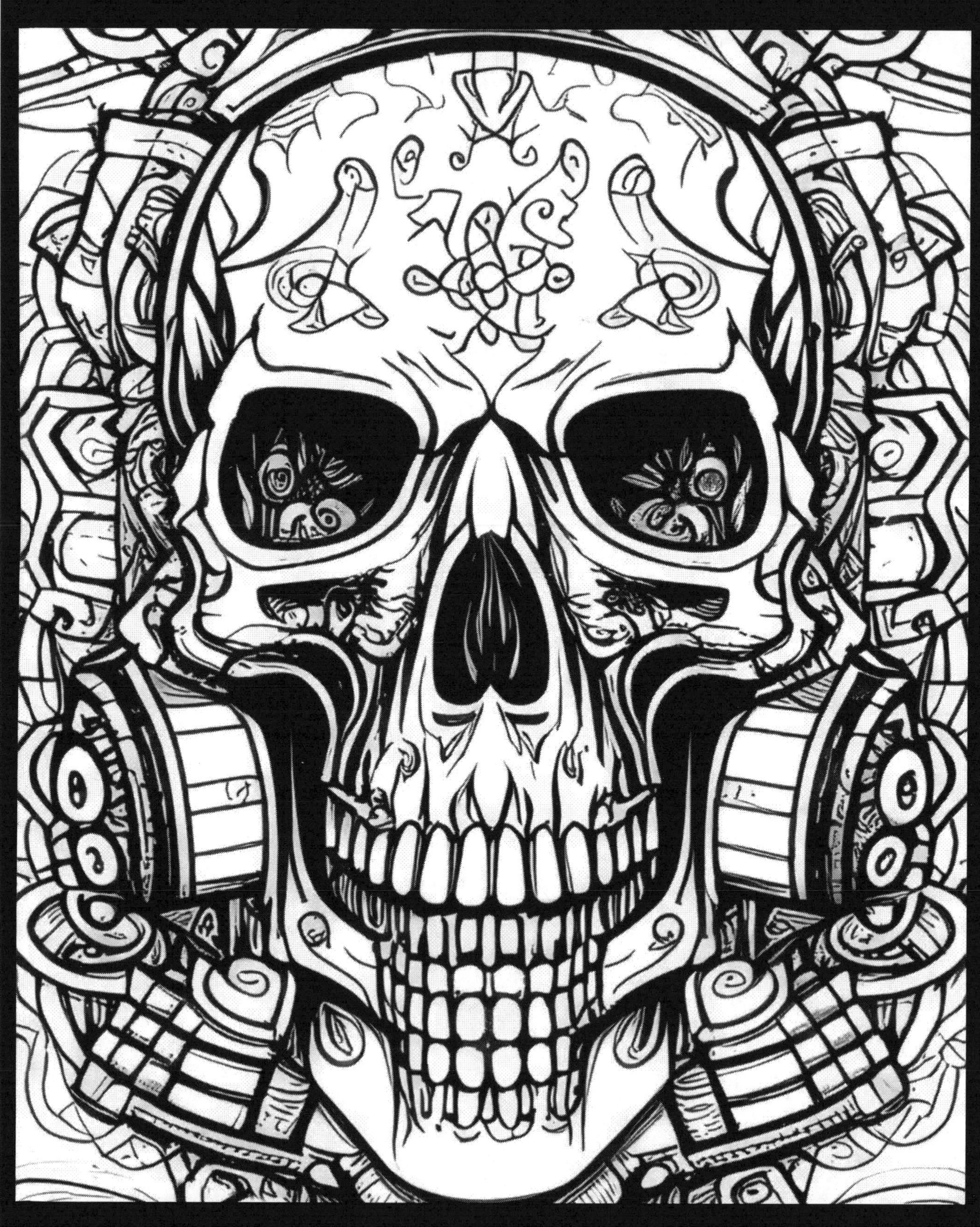

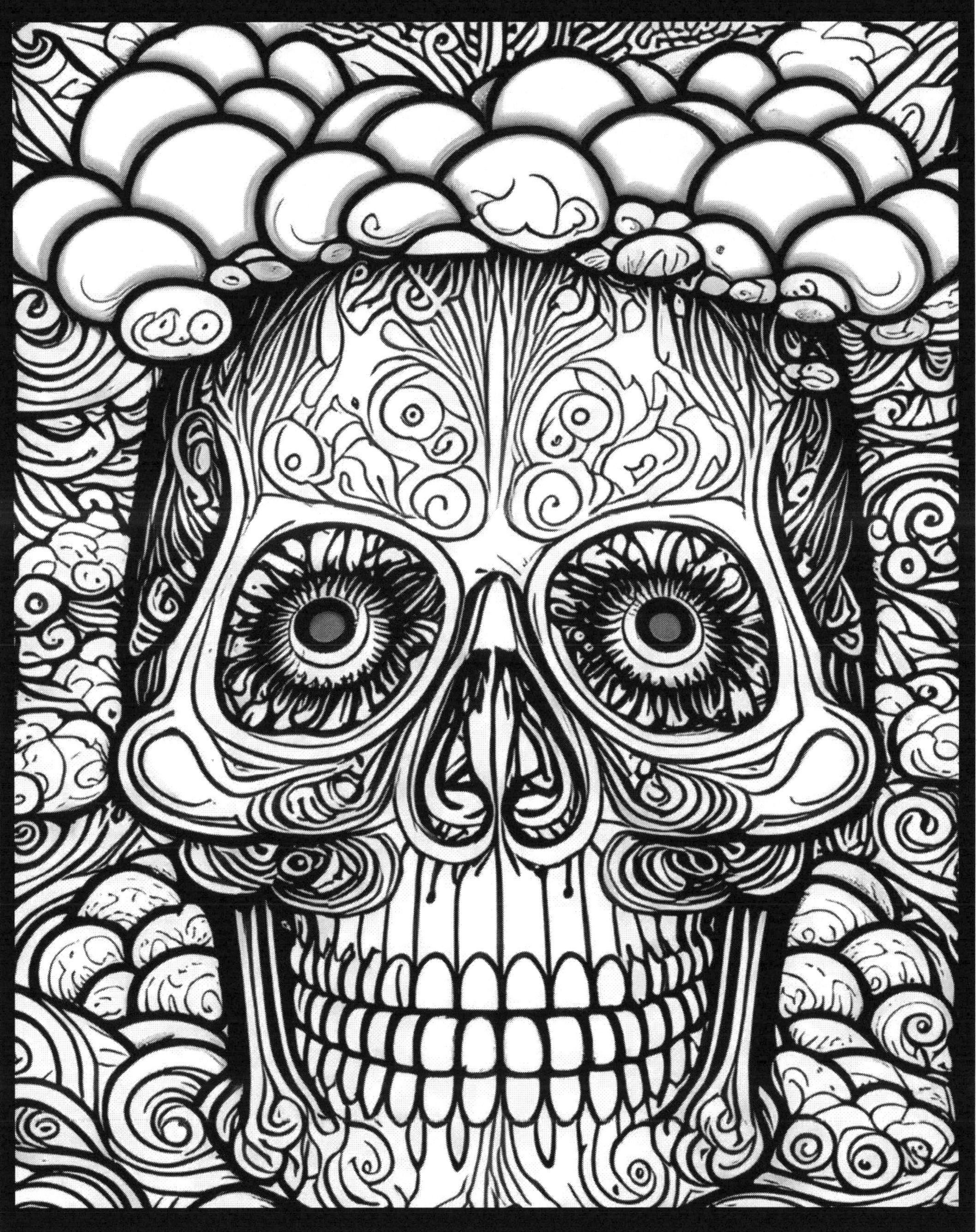

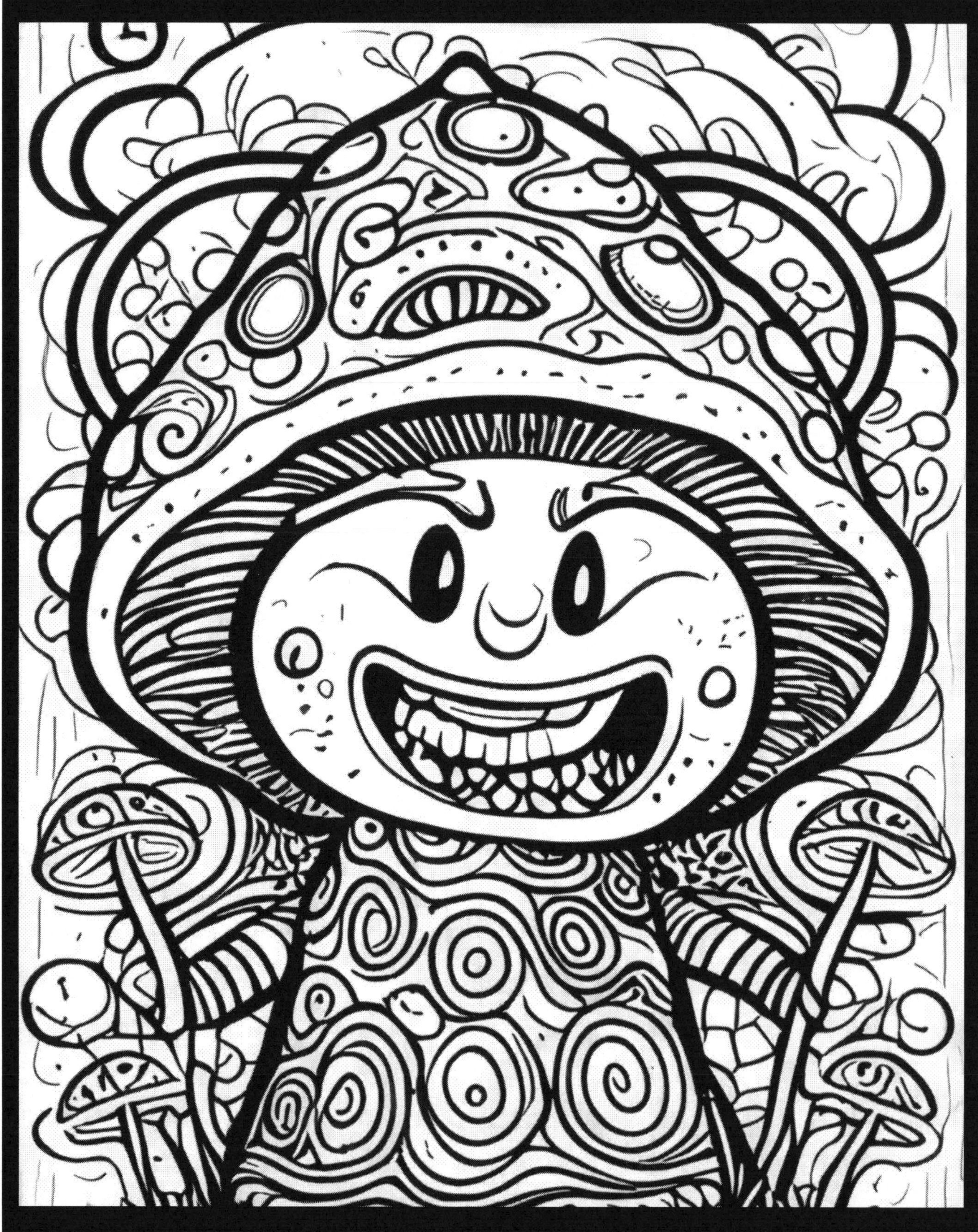

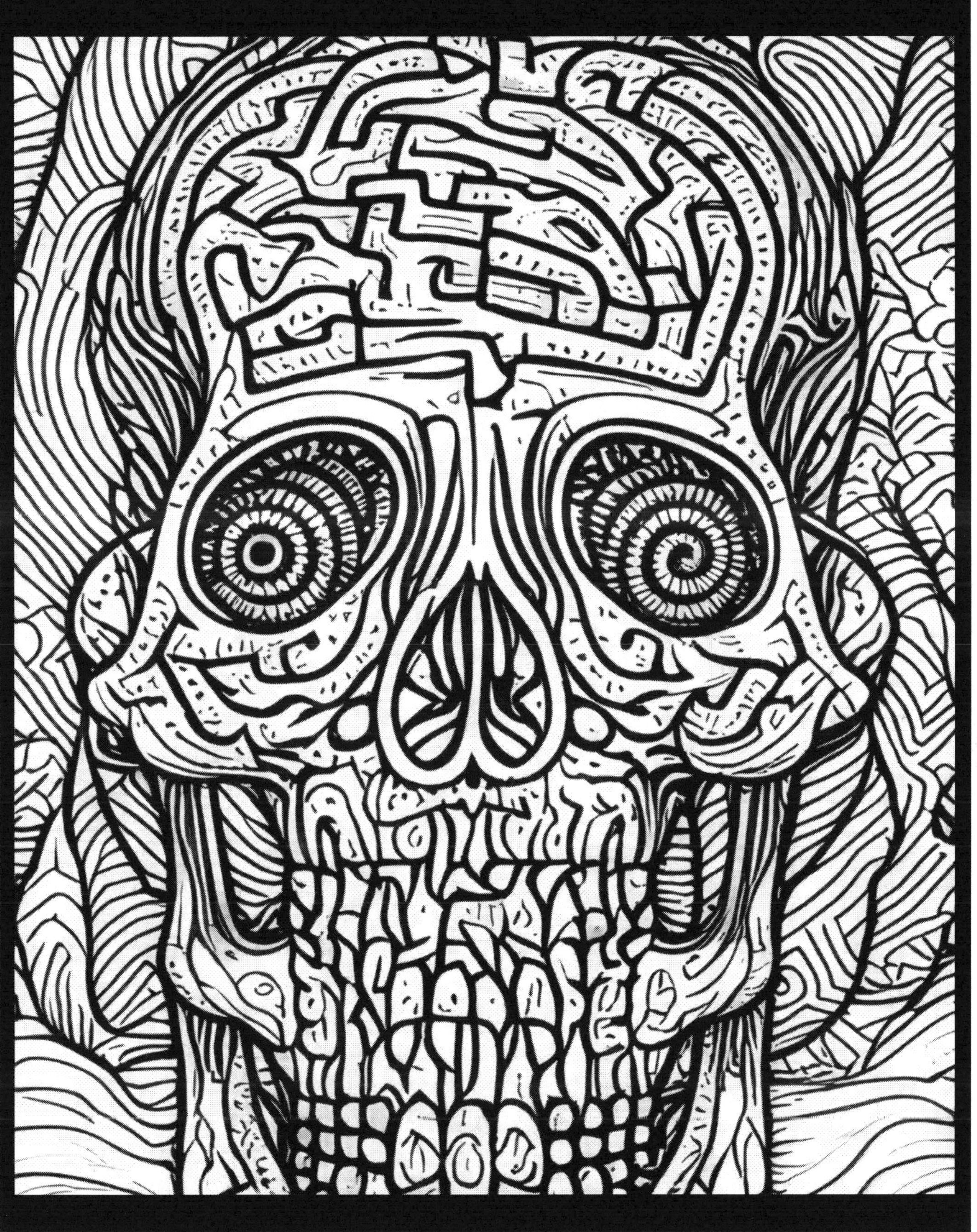

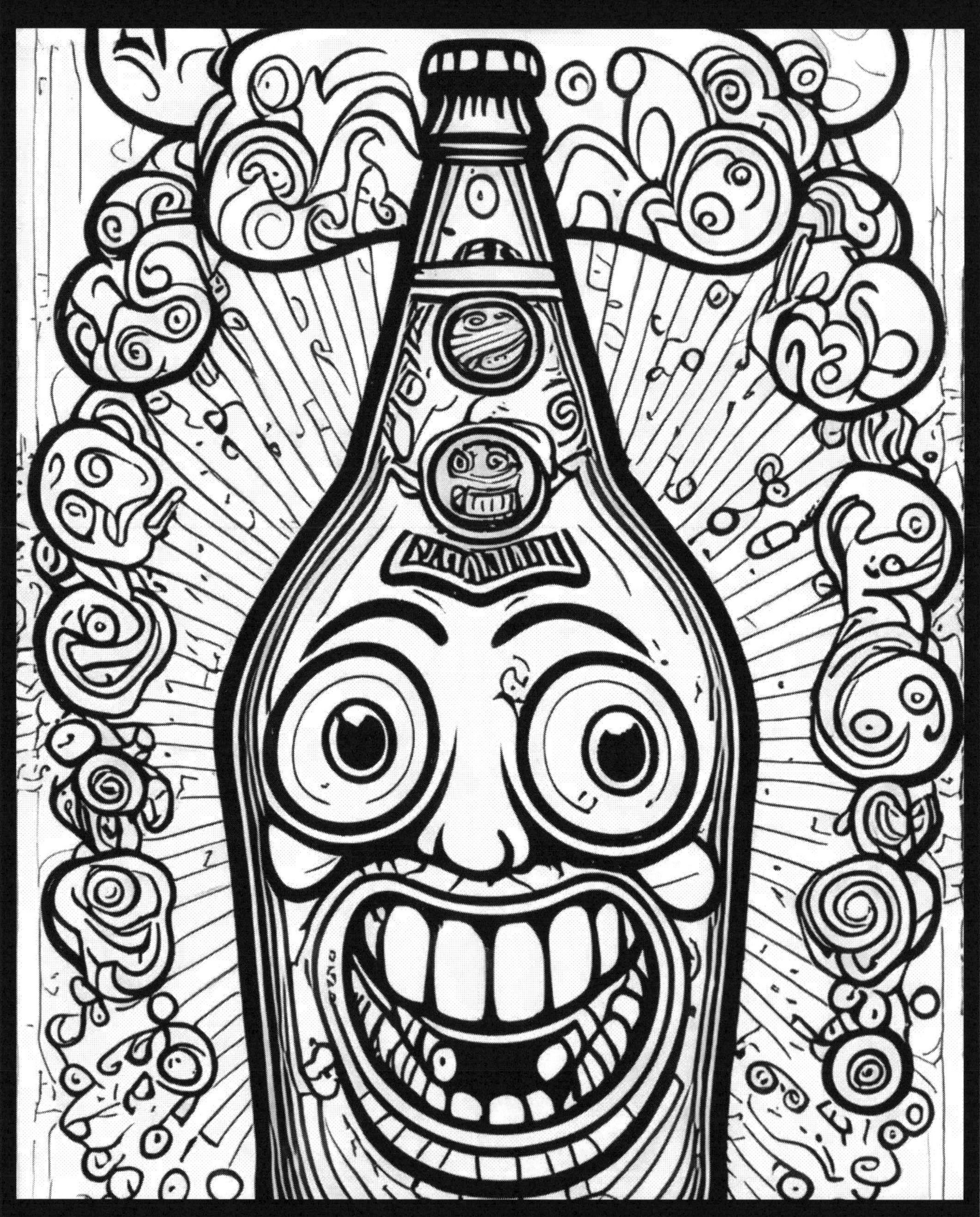

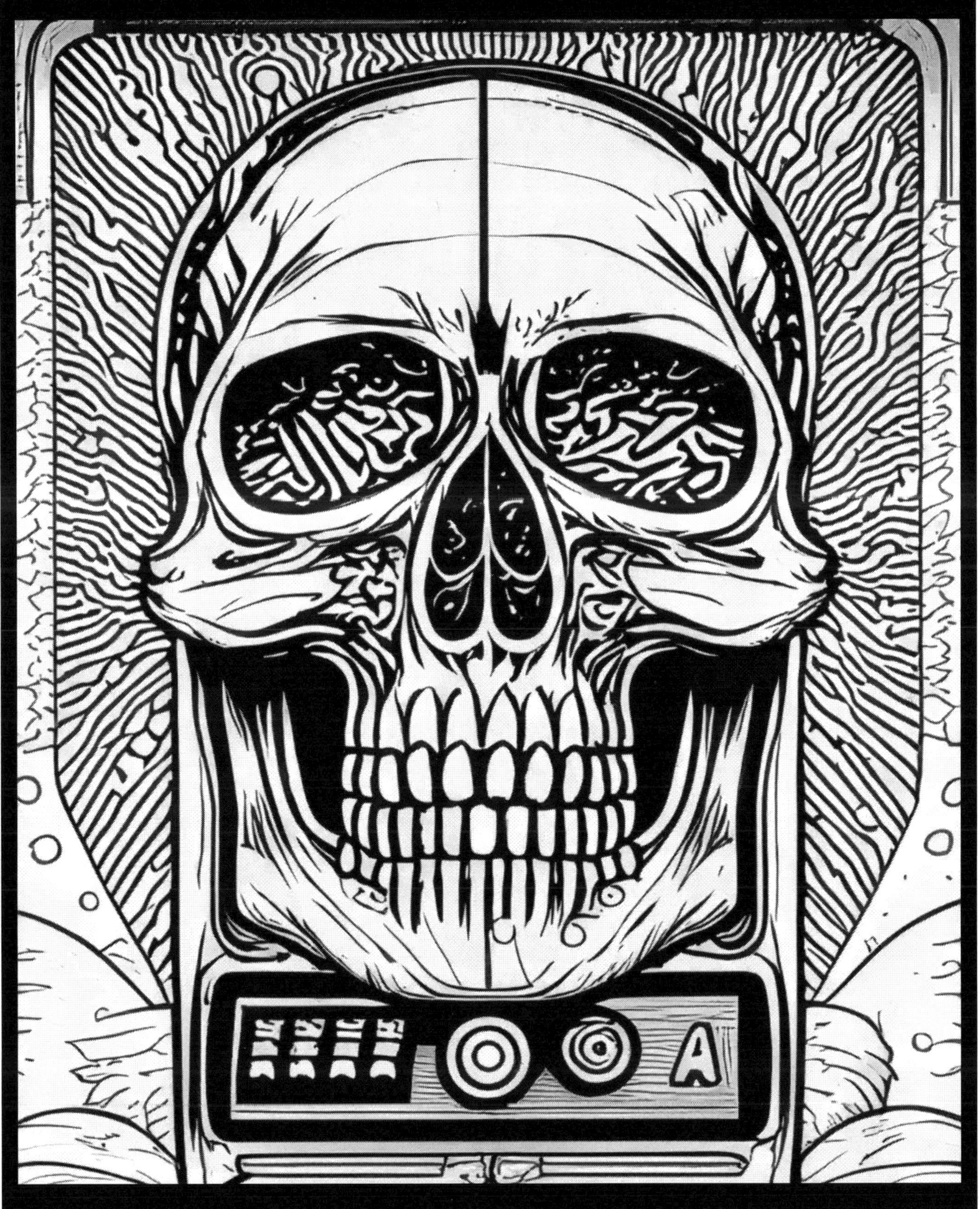
A

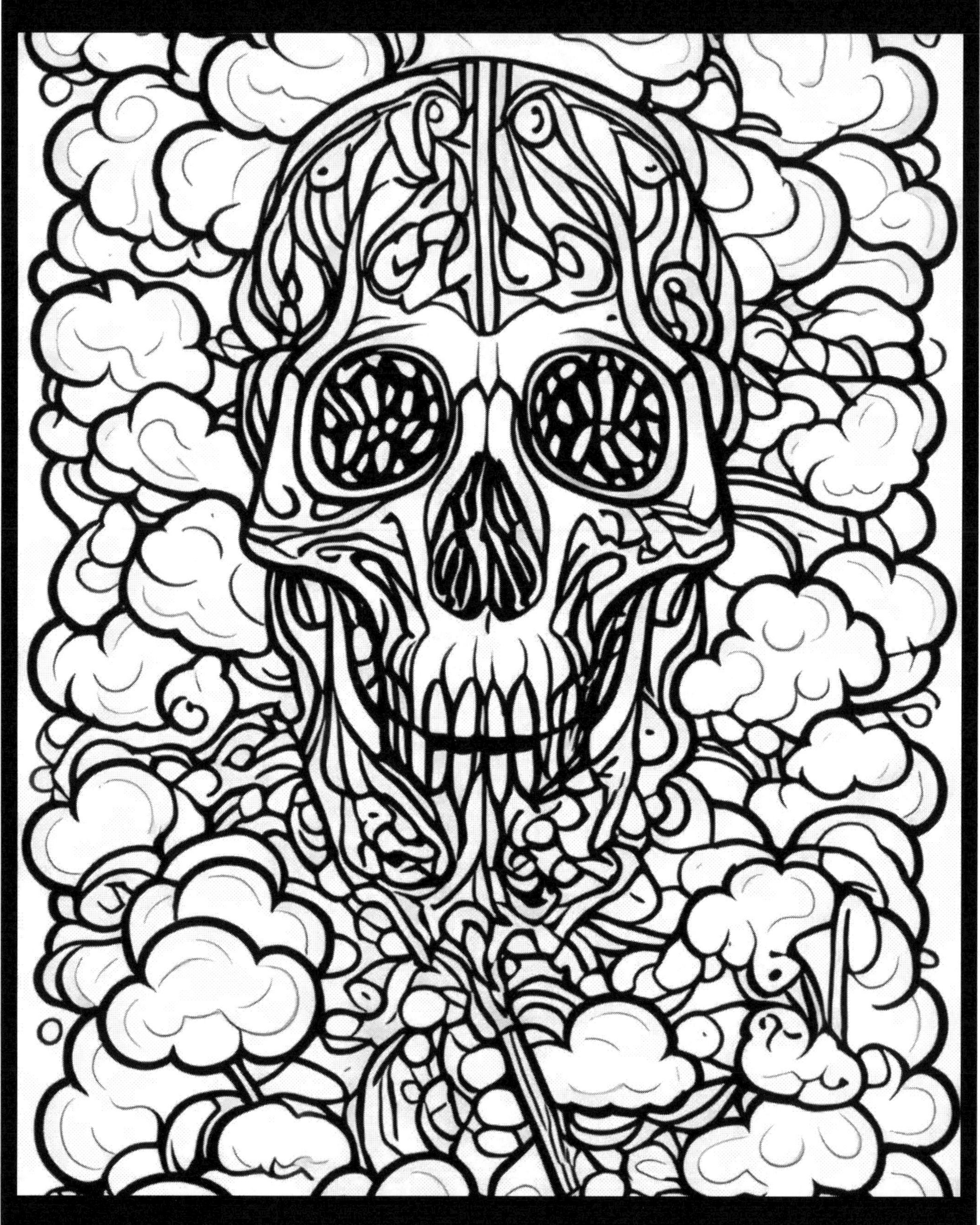

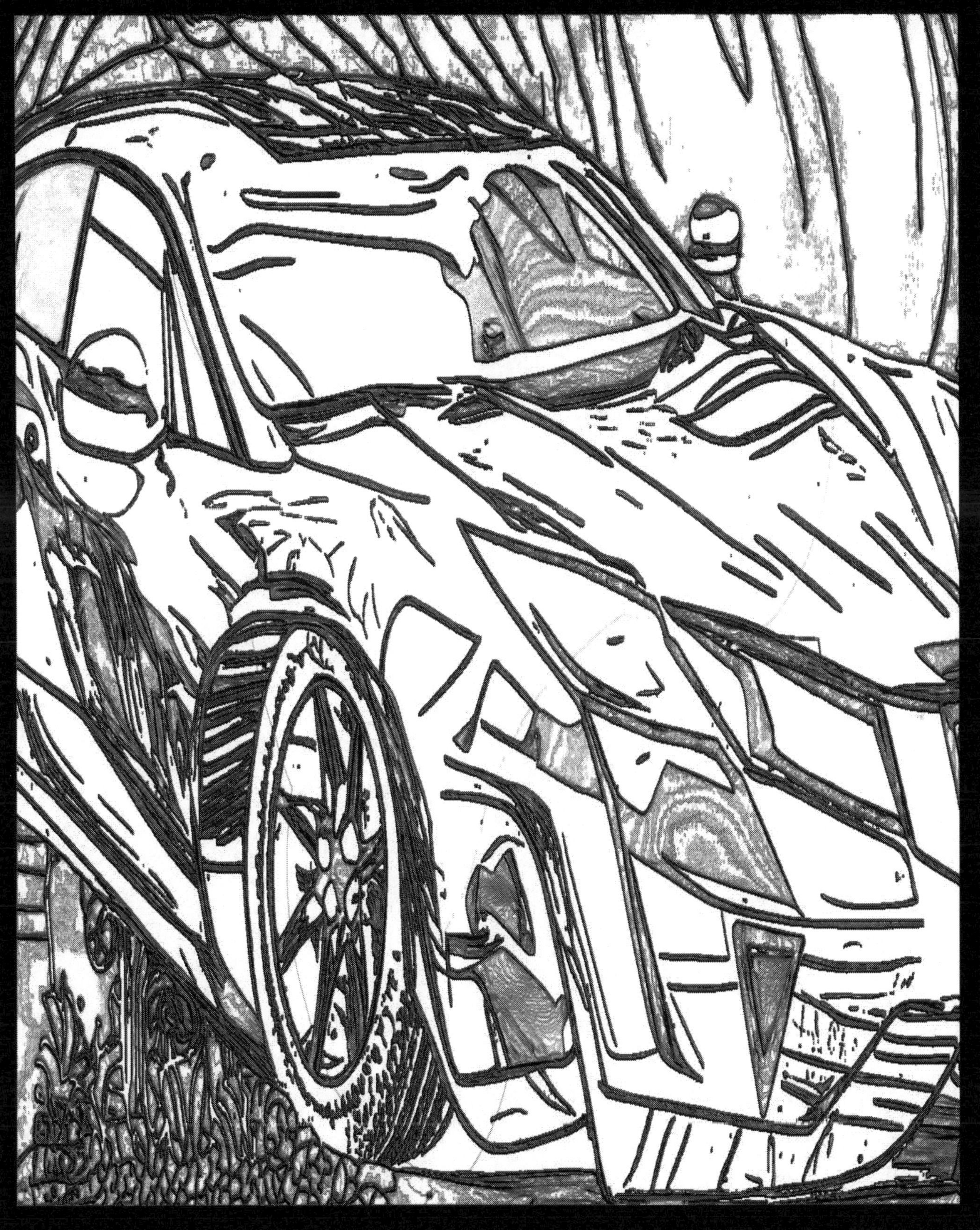

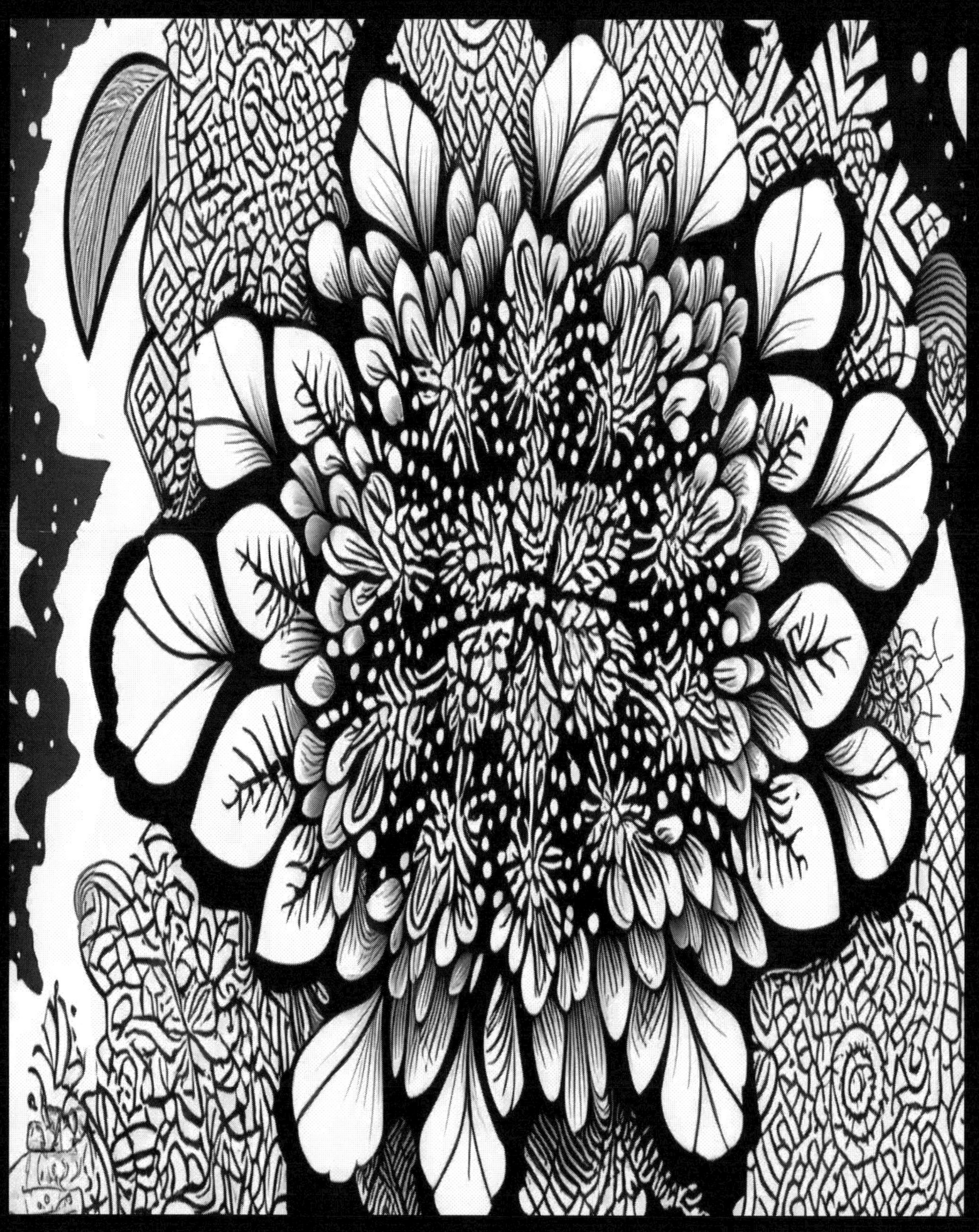

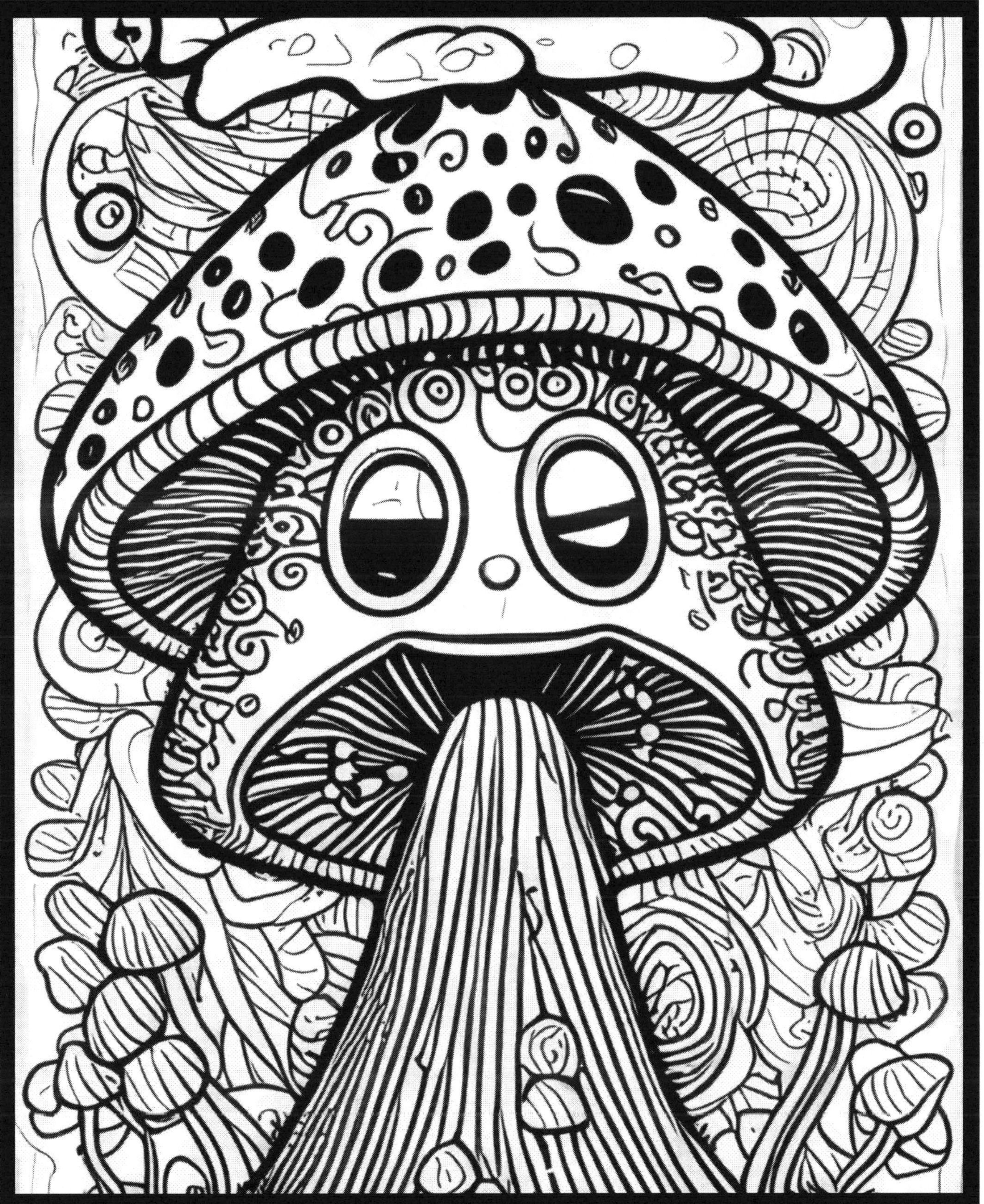

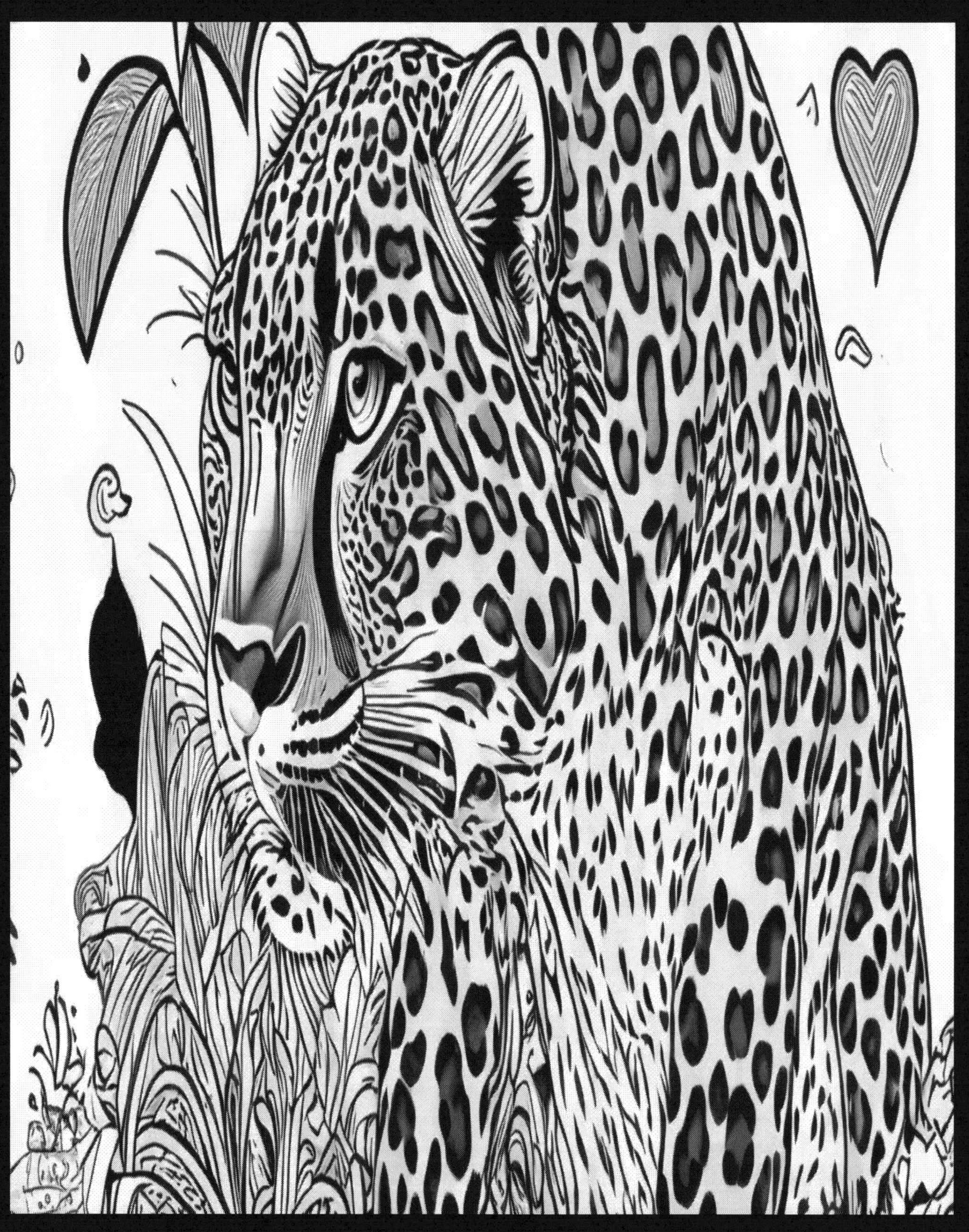

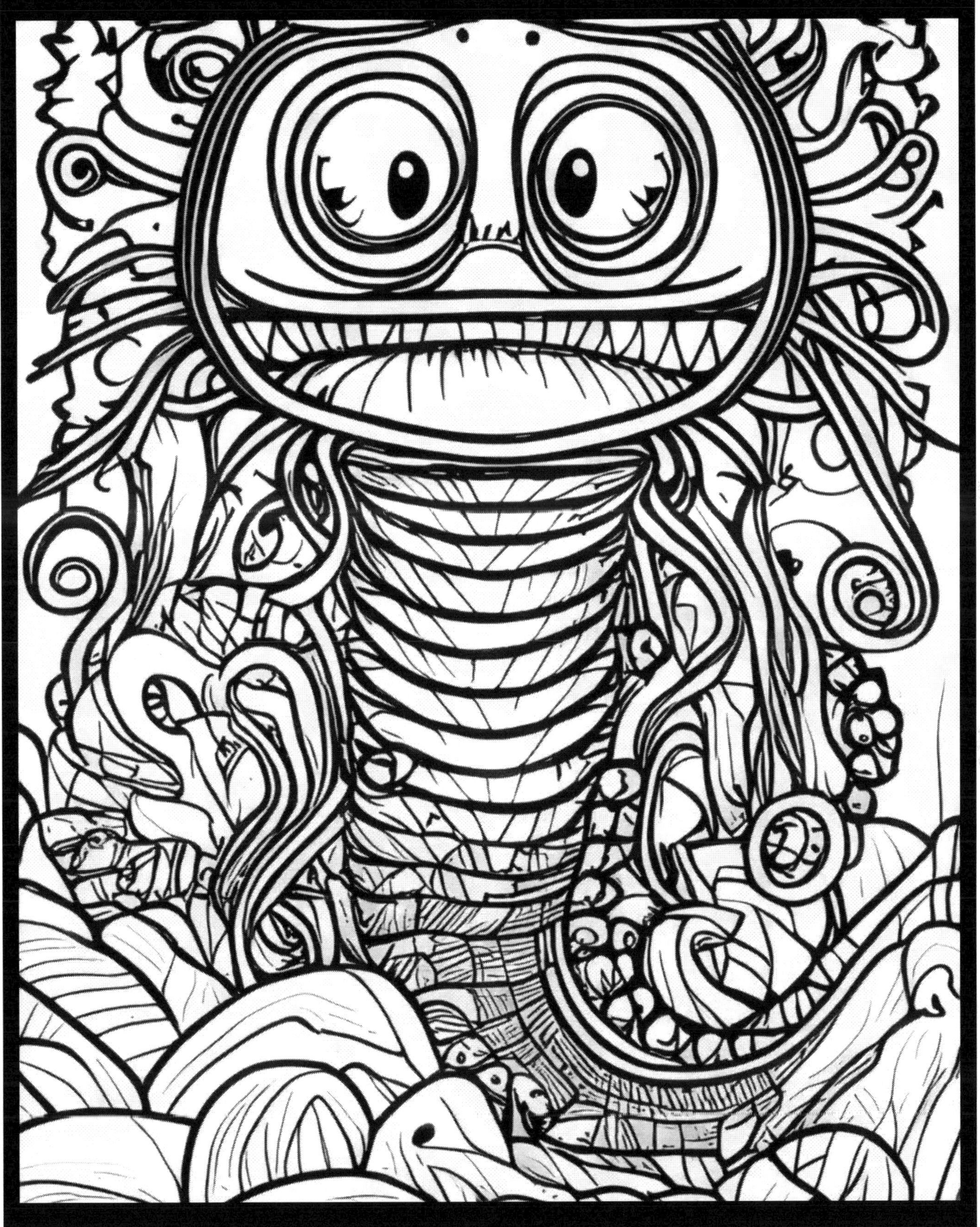

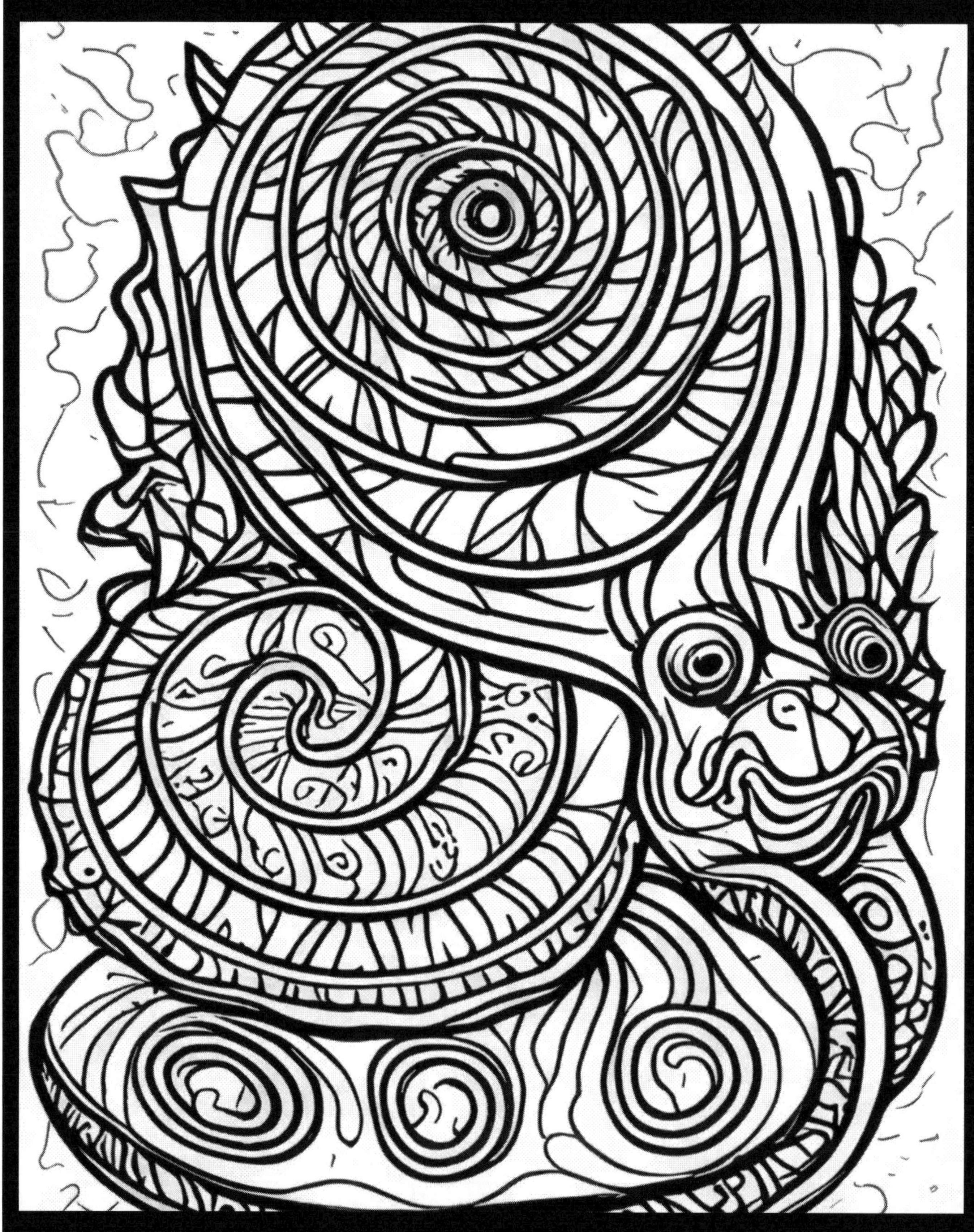

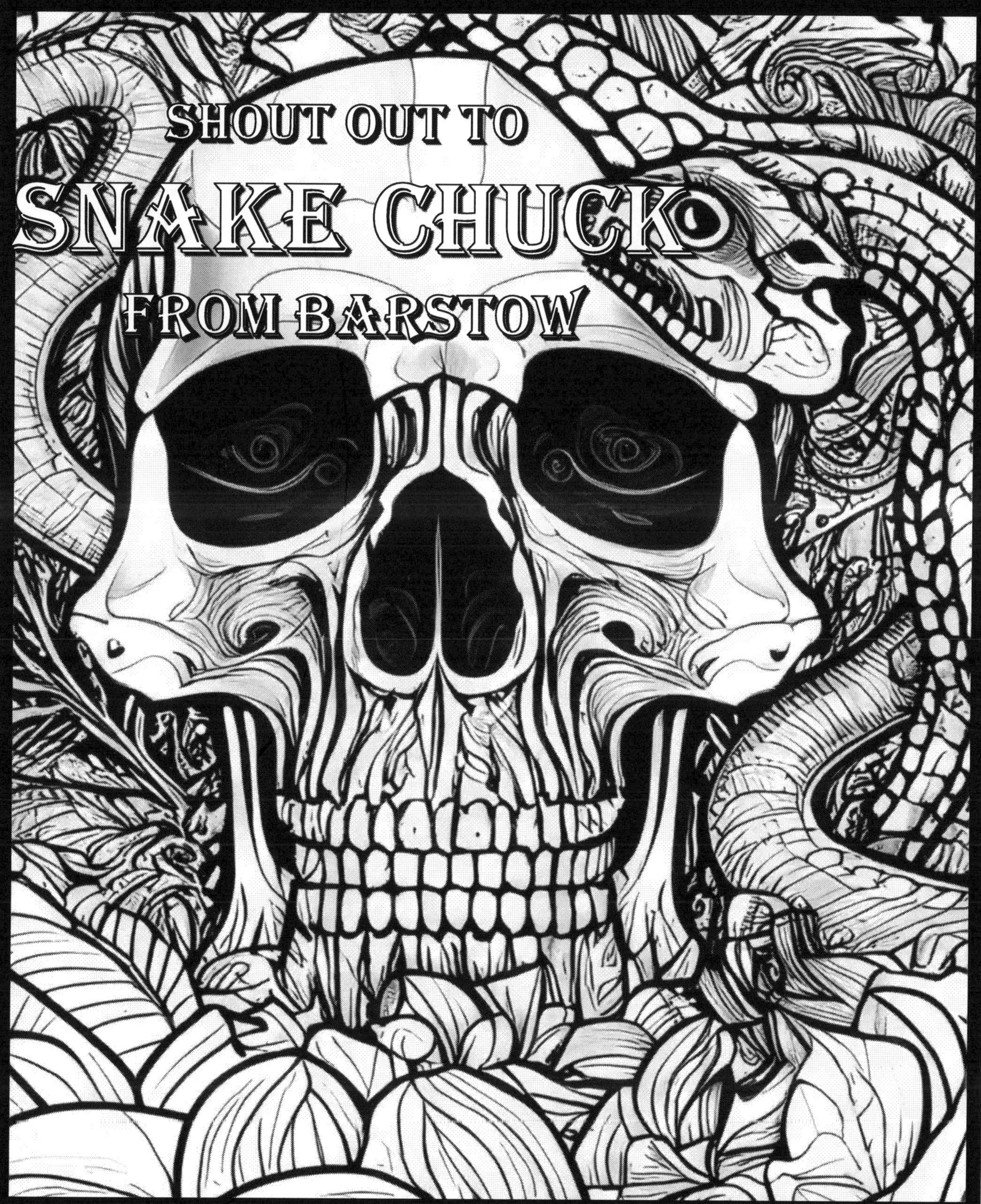
SHOUT OUT TO
SNAKE CHUCK
FROM BARSTOW

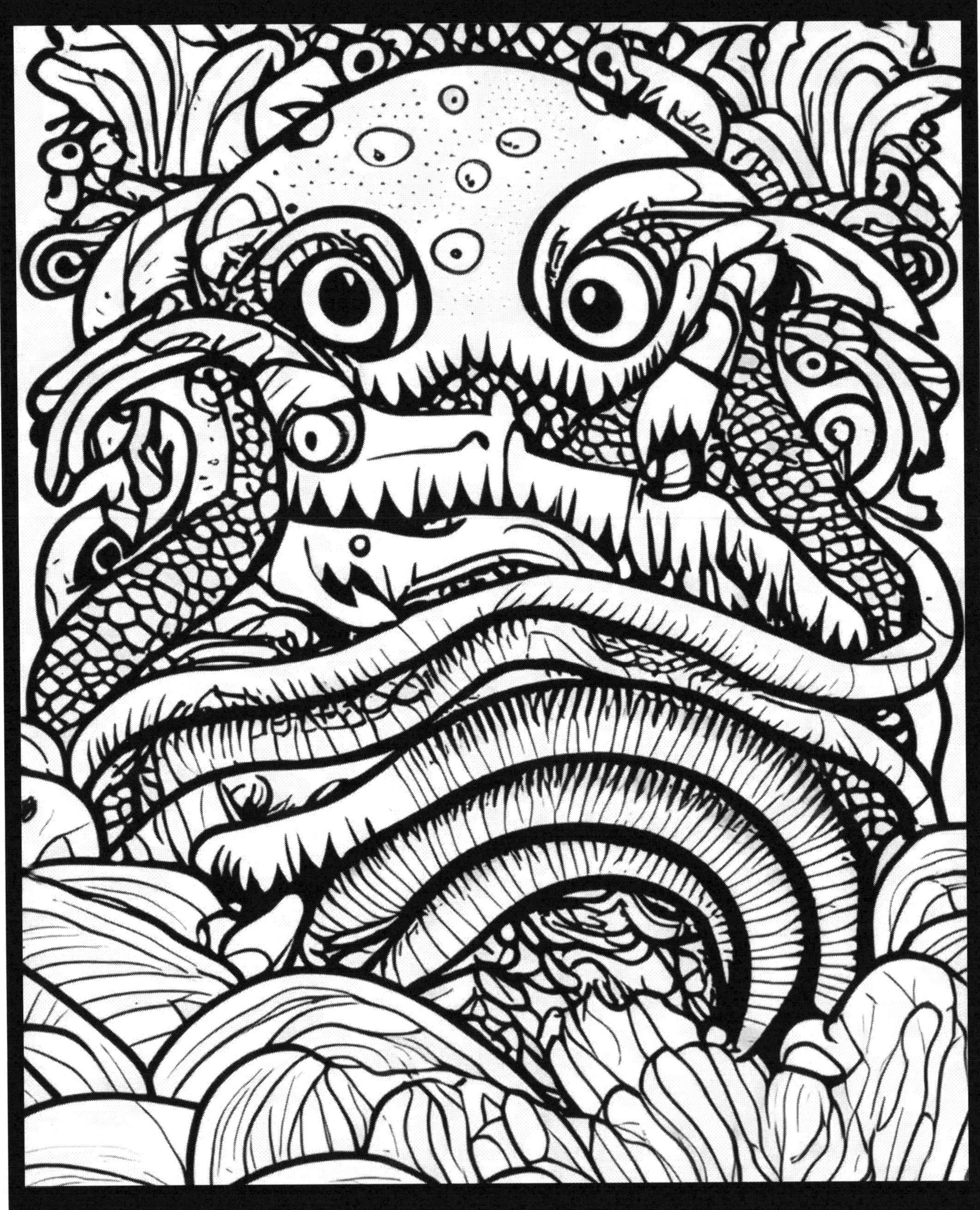

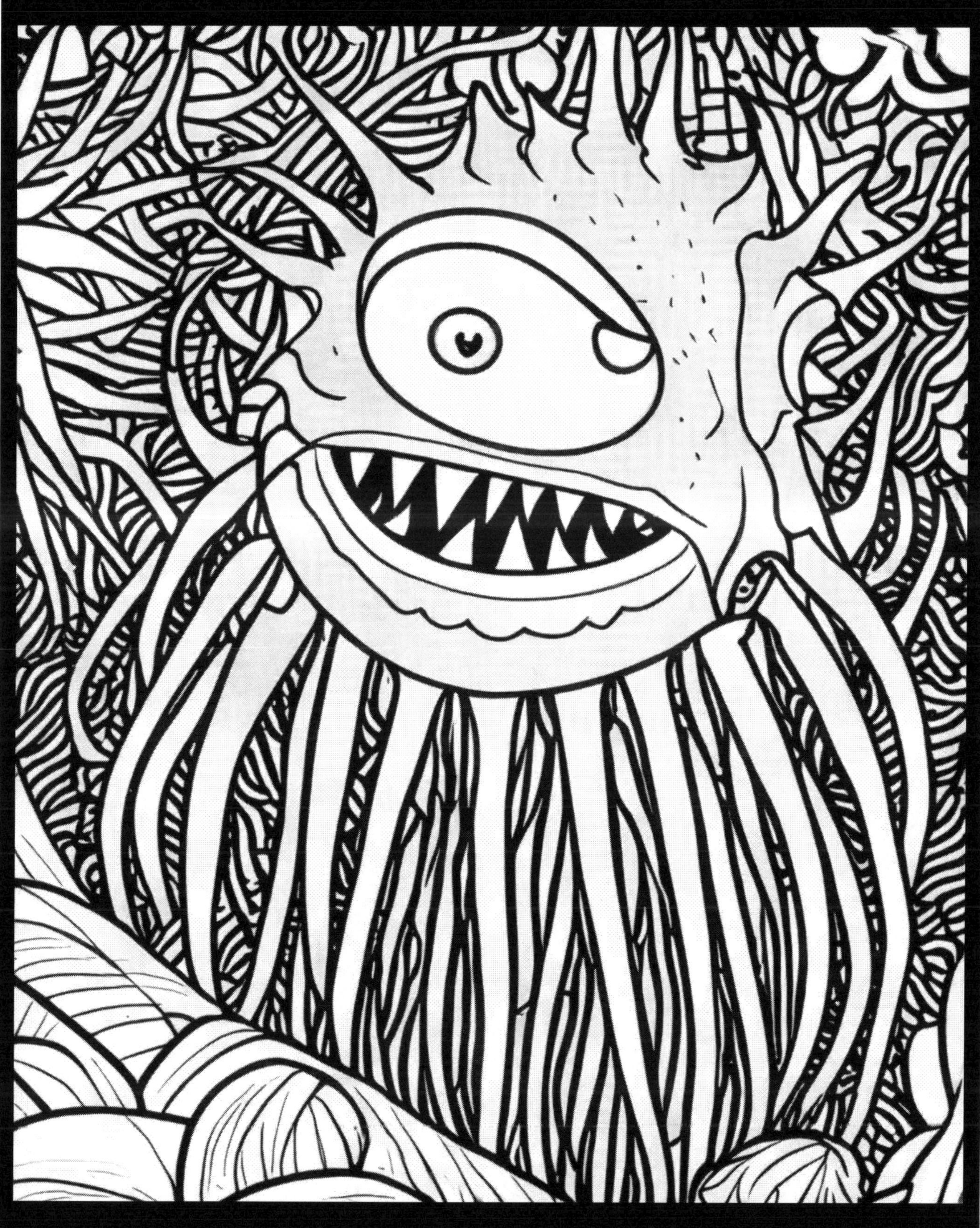

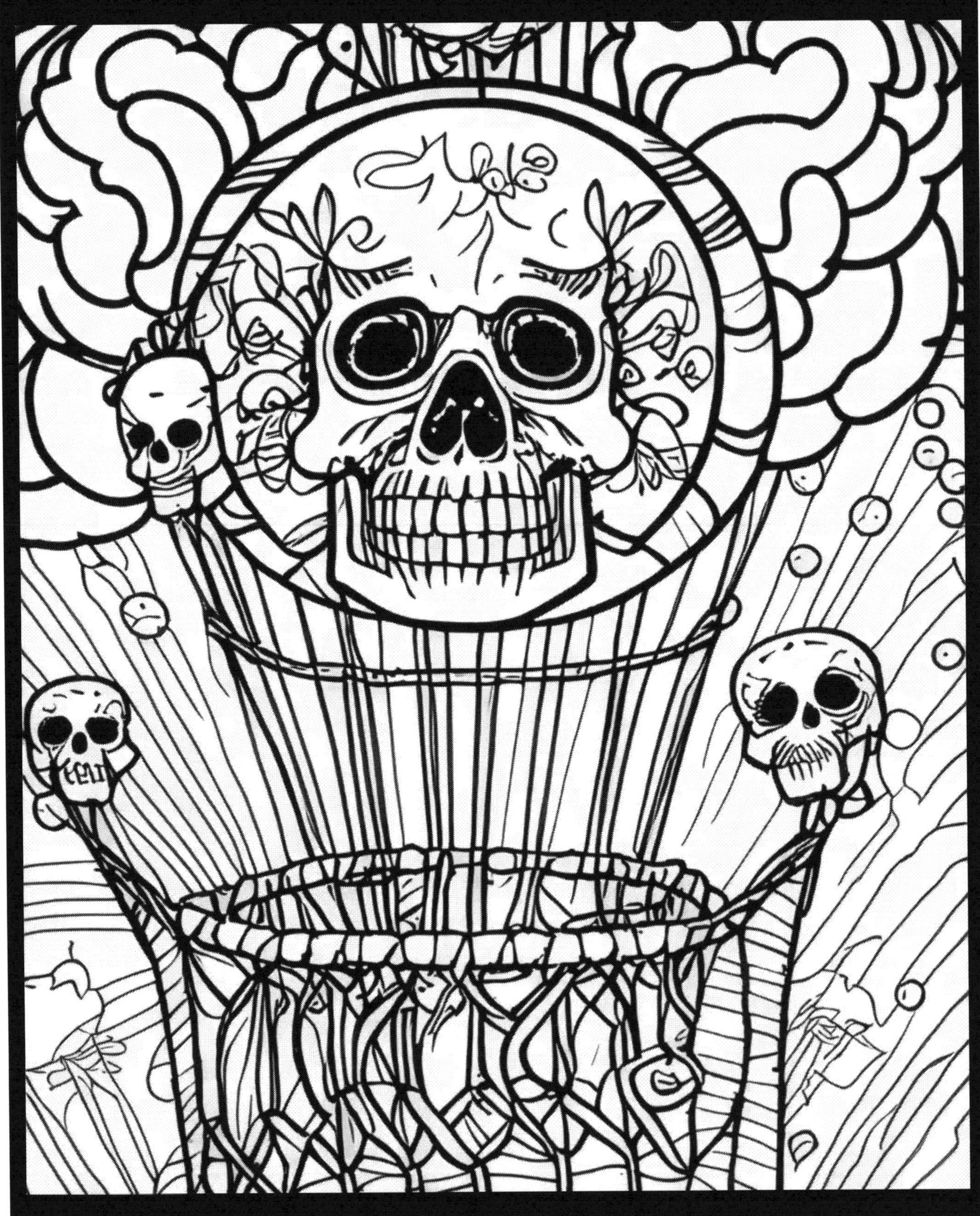

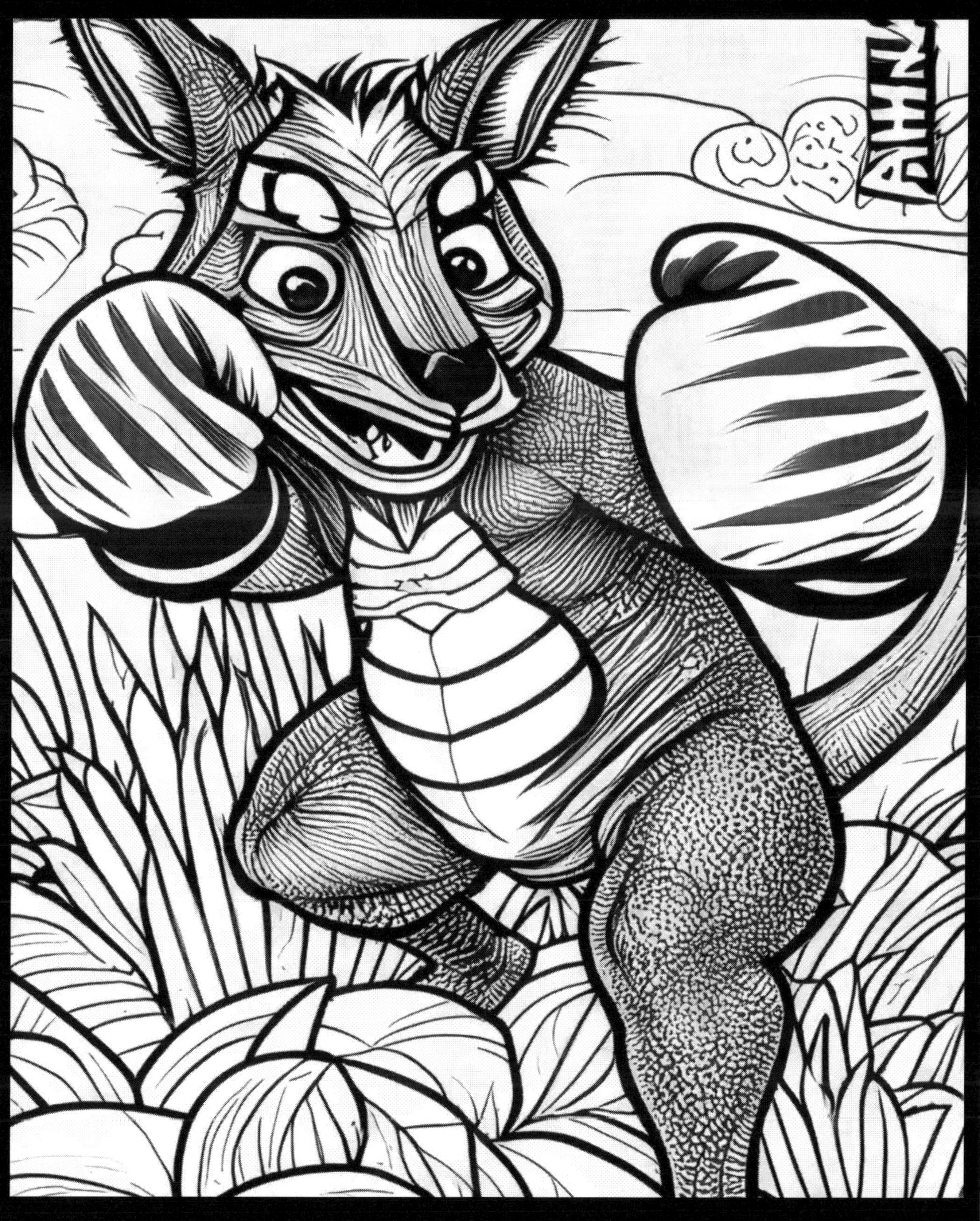

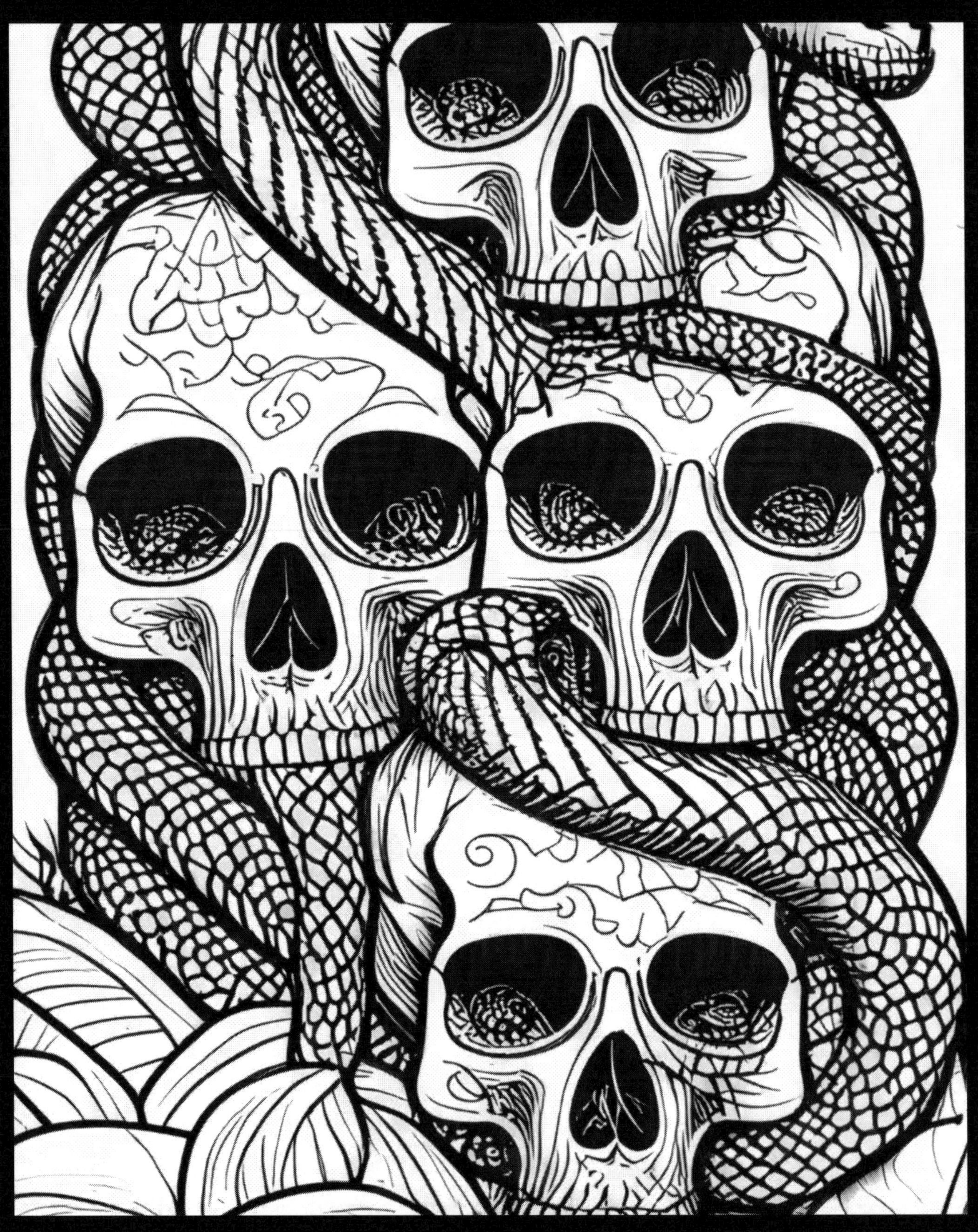

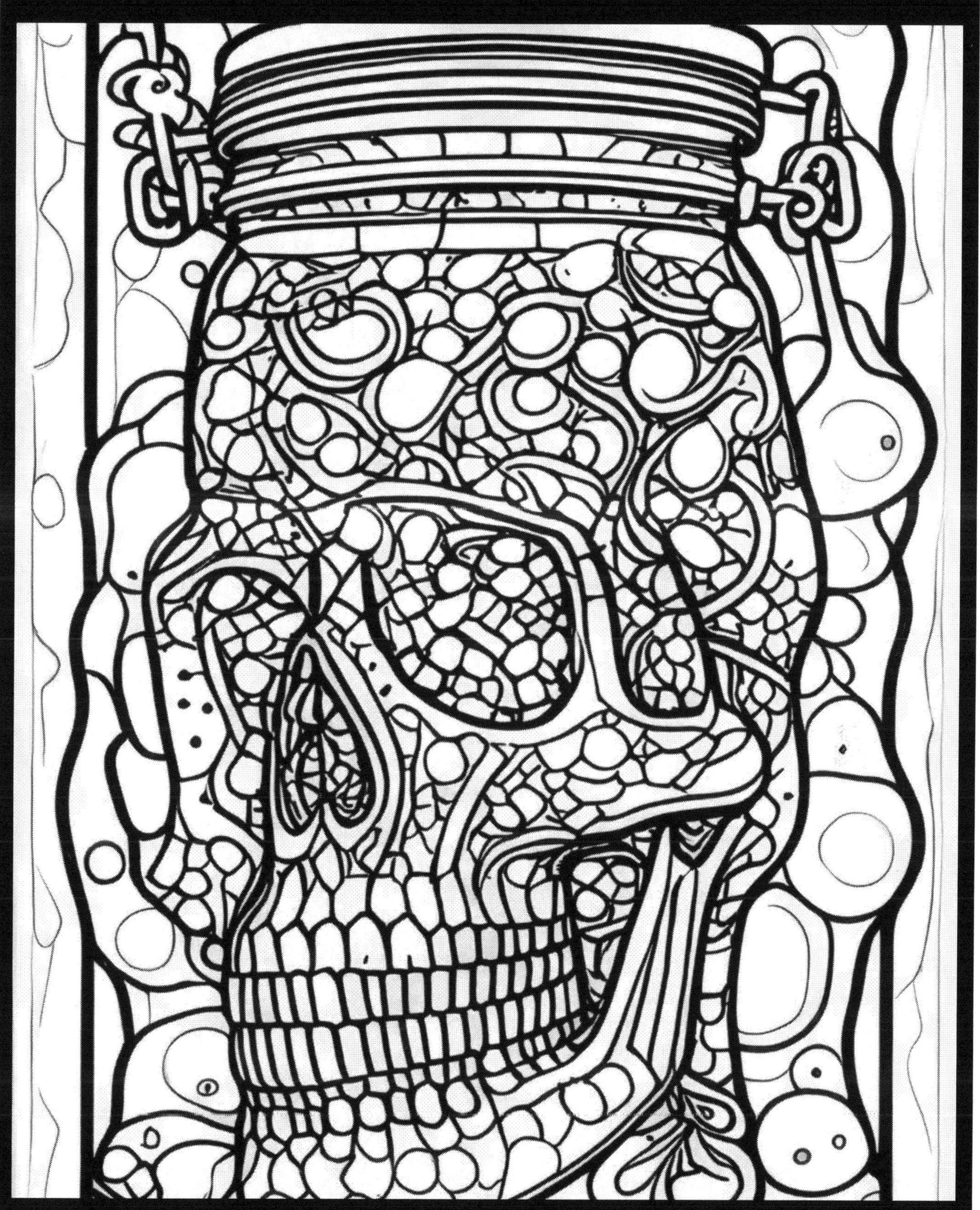

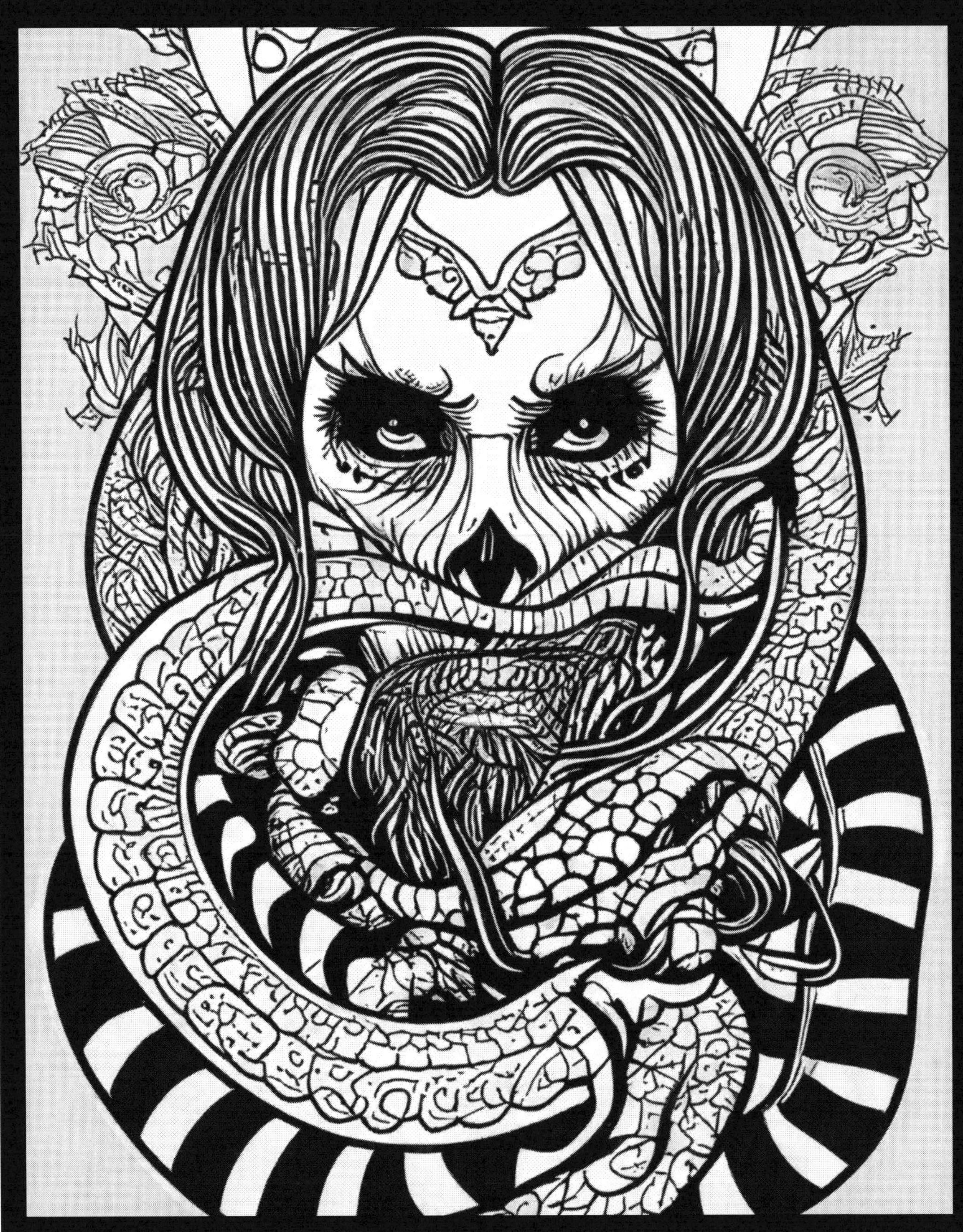

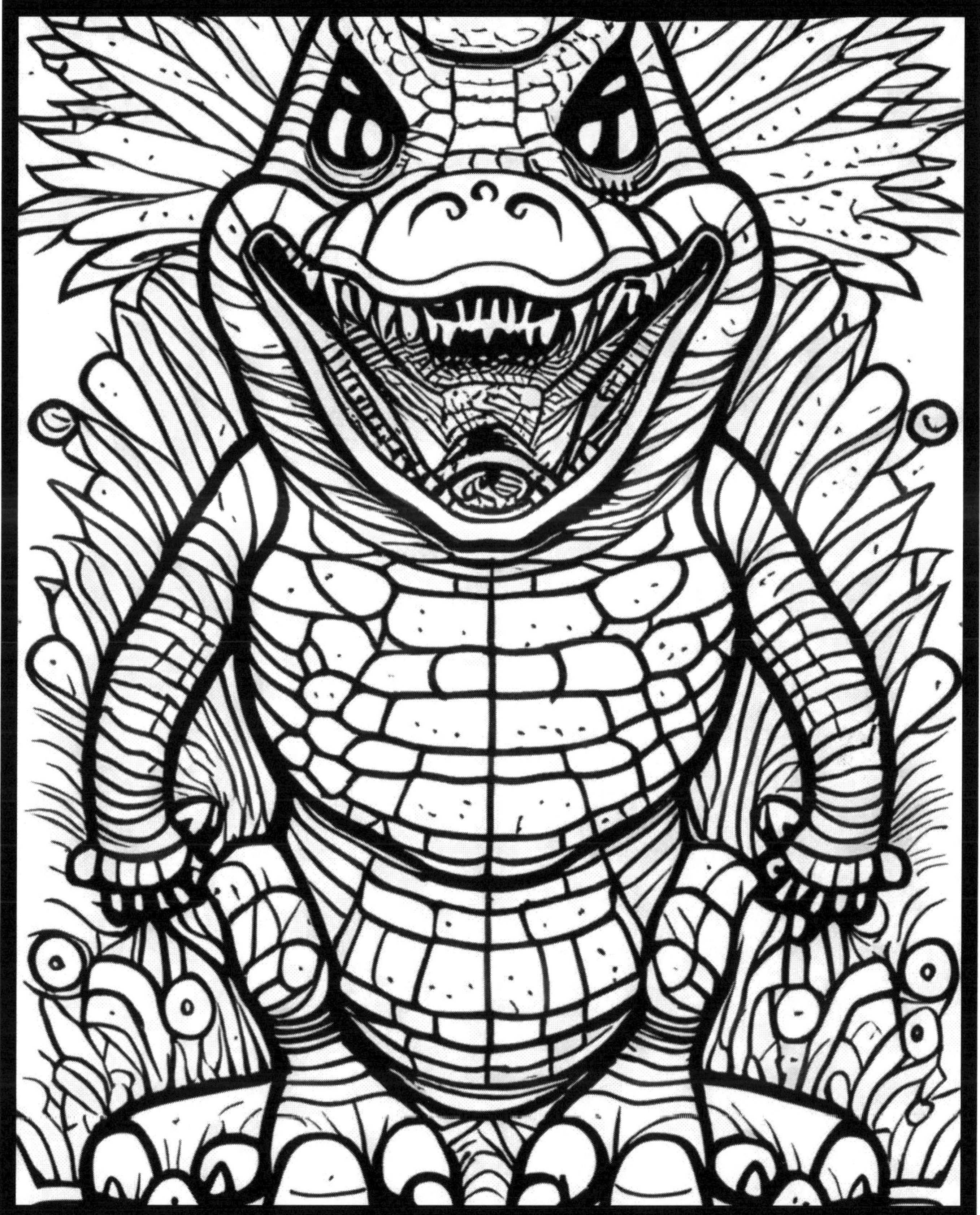

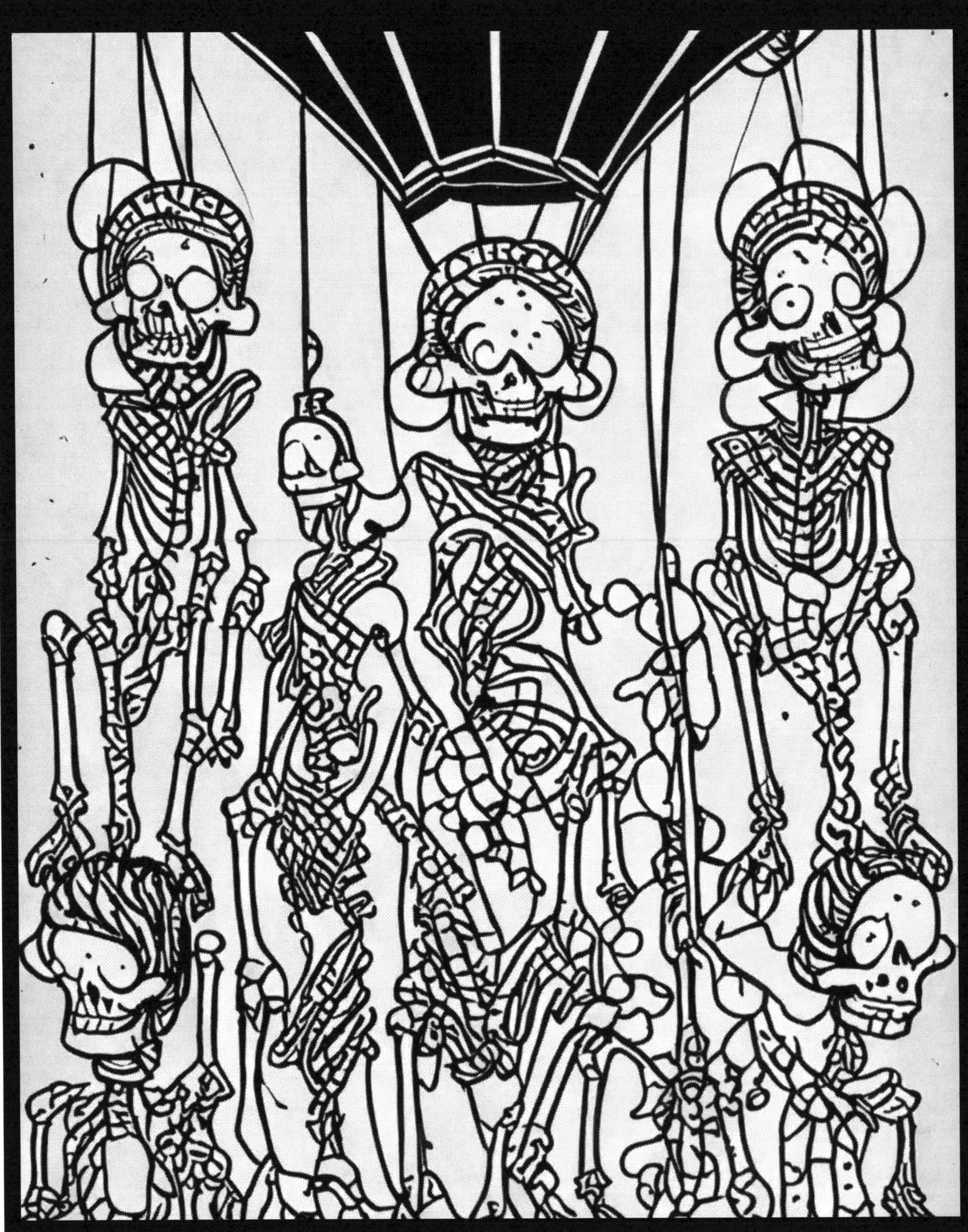

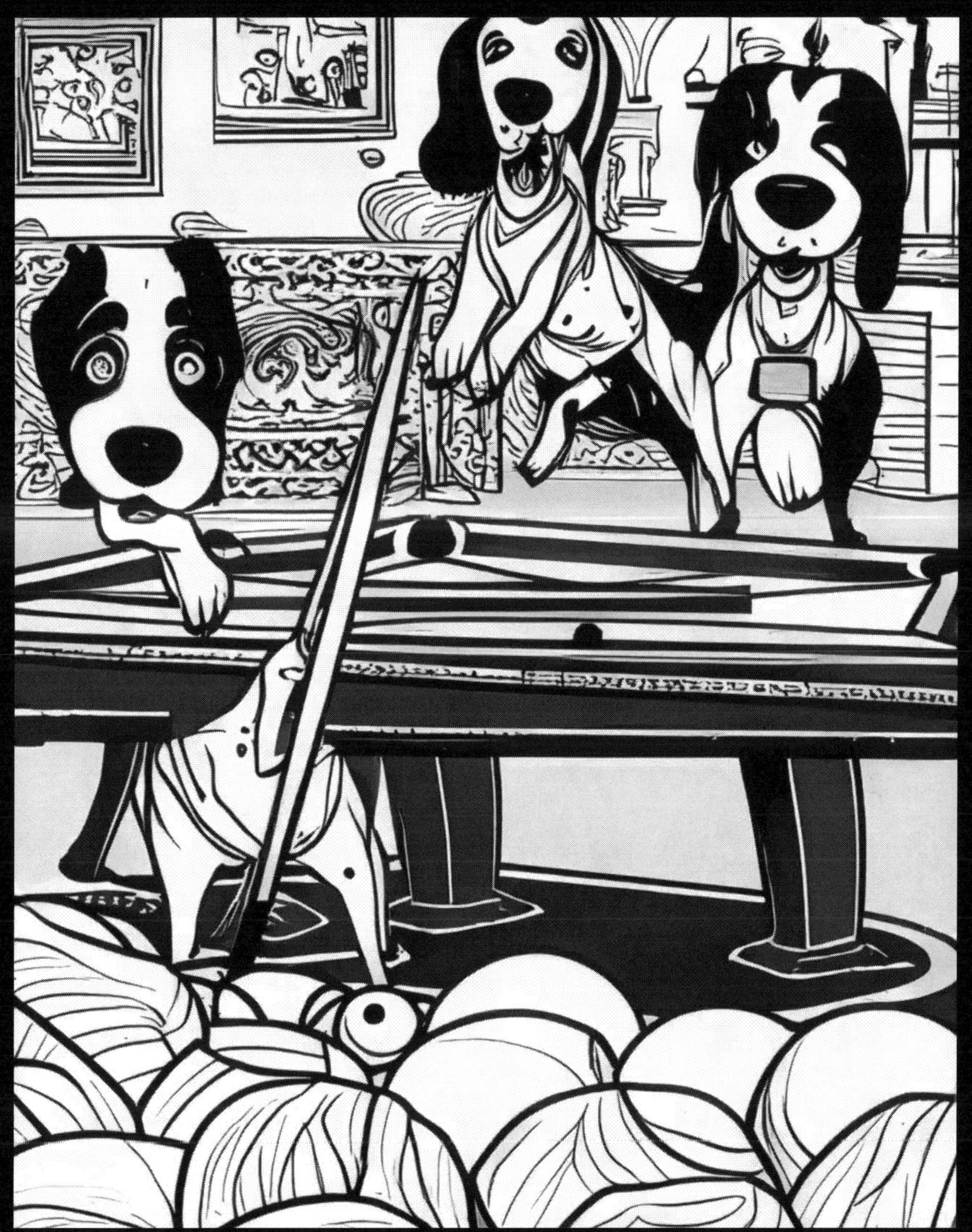

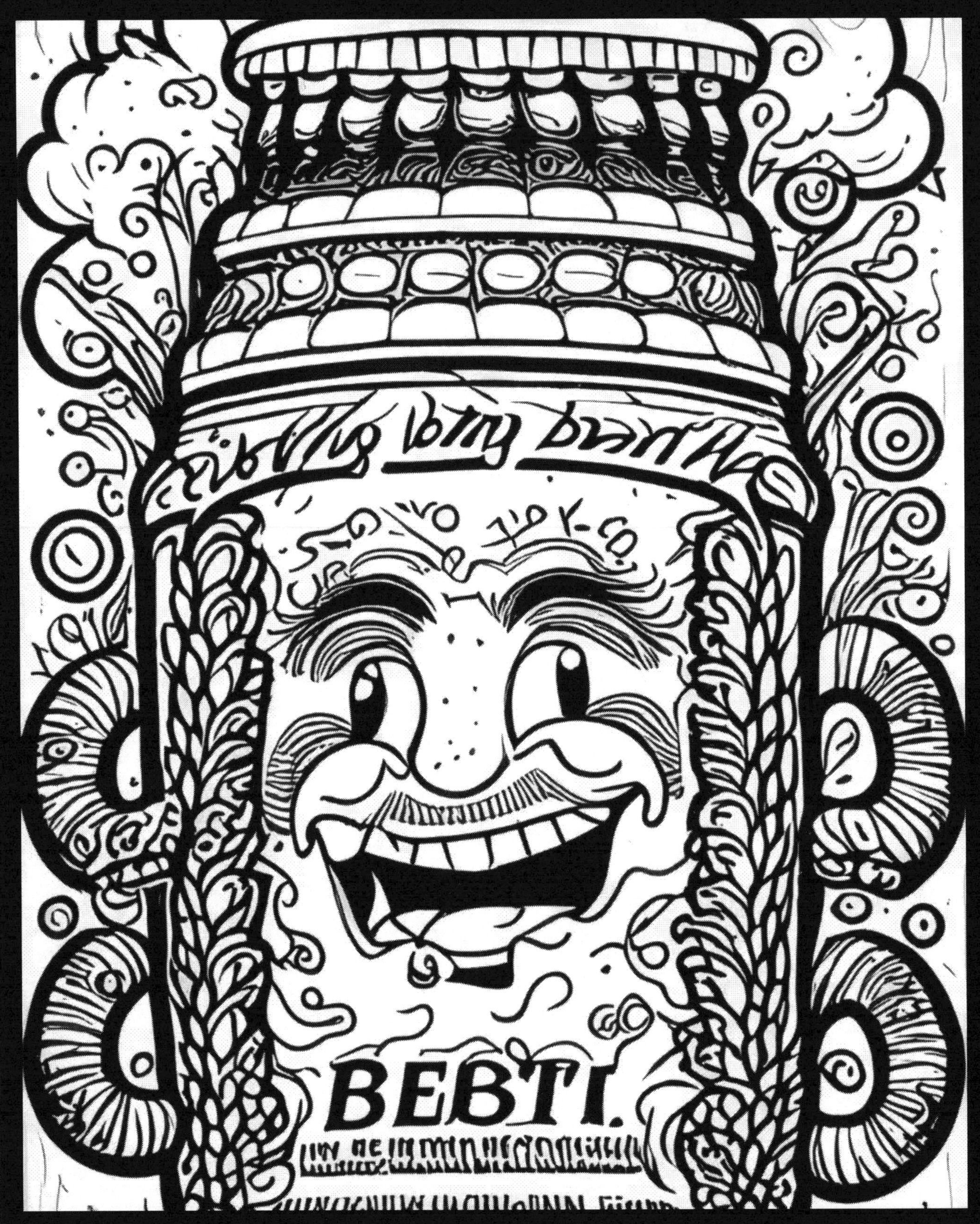
BEBTI.

Made in the USA
Middletown, DE
15 March 2024

51012147R00015